Presented to

_____

By

_____

On the Occasion of

_____

Date

_____

DAILY WISDOM
for
WORKING
WOMEN

Encouragement for Every Day

MICHELLE MEDLOCK ADAMS
AND GENA MASELLI

BARBOUR

All Scripture quotations, unless otherwise indicated, are taken from the
HOLY BIBLE, NEW INTERNATIONAL VERSION®. NIV®. Copyright © 1973,
1978, 1984 by International Bible Society. Used by permission of
Zondervan Publishing House. All rights reserved.

Scripture quotations marked KJV are taken from the King James Version of
the Bible.

Scripture quotations marked NASB are taken from the New American
Standard Bible, © 1960, 1962, 1963, 1968, 1971, 1972, 1973, 1975, 1977
by the Lockman Foundation. Used by permission.

Scripture quotations marked MSG are taken from *THE MESSAGE*. Copyright
© by Eugene H. Peterson, 1993, 1994, 1995. Used by permission of
NavPress Publishing Group.

Scripture quotations marked NLT are taken from the *Holy Bible,* New Living
Translation, copyright © 1996. Used by permission of Tyndale House
Publishers, Inc. Wheaton, Illinois 60189, U.S.A. All rights reserved.

Design: UDG | DesignWorks, Sisters, Oregon—
Cover: Christopher Gilbert; Interior: Robin Black

Published by Barbour Publishing, Inc., P.O. Box 719, Uhrichsville, Ohio
44683, www.barbourbooks.com

*Our mission is to publish and distribute inspirational products offering
exceptional value and biblical encouragement to the masses.*

Member of the
Evangelical Christian
Publishers Association

Printed in China.
5 4 3 2 1

*For my best friend Raegan
and my sister-in-law Barb—
wonderful elementary schoolteachers
and a credit to today's working women.
I love you both!
Michelle (A.K.A. Missy)*

*To Patricia Irene Heinen and Alice Williams Pfeifer,
the most inspiring and hardest working women
I've ever known.
Gena*

DELIVERING THE MAIL

If the LORD delights in a man's way,
he makes his steps firm.

PSALM 37:23

D o you remember the first "career" position you held? Just thinking about mine keeps me *very* humble. After numerous interviews and months of temp work, I finally landed my first professional position as a marketing assistant, responsible for helping the marketing supervisor. Within weeks of my arrival, my new boss, who had never before had an assistant, gained added responsibilities and became a one-woman, cracker-jack show. She did everything for herself. My days, on the other hand, dragged. My daily highlight became delivering the mail. Sadly, it was the one ten-minute task I had to do.

Thankfully, four months later I was promoted. Because of the things I'd learned, such as the department's procedures and vision, I was prepared to do more. I learned that every step is a preparation for the next.

If you're in a position and you think, *I could do so much more!* don't despair. God hasn't forgotten you; the skills you're learning *will* be put to a good use. Until then, be patient and learn all you can. As you trust God, He *will* make your steps firm. —GM

POWER PRAYER
Lord, I'm thankful for my job because I know You use it to meet my needs. As I prepare for promotion, I trust You with every area of my life.

Change Is in the Air

"He changes times and seasons;
he sets up kings and deposes them. He gives wisdom
to the wise and knowledge to the discerning."

Daniel 2:21

Change is coming. . .you can sense it. Perhaps it's a job. A relationship. A volunteer ministry. Something. Anything. And that's exciting! It's as if a beautiful Christmas present has been placed under the tree with your name on it. You're just waiting for the perfect time to unwrap it and peek inside.

The best part about these times is that you are once again reminded that God is working on your behalf. He thinks enough of you to direct you to another job or bring a new relationship into your life. It's one more reminder that you are special to Him.

Of course, until the day arrives when you know exactly what the change is, you have to be patient, consistently doing what you know to do. Then just watch God direct you, and pray for insight. You're not alone. The God of the universe—the Beginning and the End—is right there working in your life. Now, isn't that comforting? –GM

POWER PRAYER
Lord, I feel impressed that You're going to do something new in my life. I thank You for it in advance and am ready to see what it is.

DISTRACTIONS

Oh, that my ways were steadfast in obeying your decrees!
PSALM 119:5

There are days when I'm set to work. I know
just want I need, to accomplish. I have
everything I need, and then suddenly. . .the phone
rings. In fact, it seems like it continues to ring all
day. And in between the phone calls, I get several
questions from coworkers. Throw in a couple of
unexpected—and unproductive—meetings and
voilà, I have a completely wasted day. I've been so
distracted that I haven't accomplished anything.

Unfortunately, distractions come in all shapes
and sizes. In the office, they're endless phone calls,
long meetings, and watercooler banter. In your
spiritual life, they may be people, fear, or the
busyness of life. Basically, they're anything that

keeps you from focusing on God and spending time with Him.

As you determine to spend time with God in prayer every day, ask Him to help you prioritize your day. As you make this a part of your life, you'll begin to understand true productivity. You'll begin to differentiate the necessary to-do list items in your life from the distractions. In time, you'll have the satisfaction of accomplishing what He's called you to do. –GM

POWER PRAYER

Dear Lord, thank You for showing me exactly what I need to do today—for You and at work—and help me to steer clear of distractions.

An Honest Day's Work

Moses inspected the work and saw that
they had done it just as the LORD had commanded.
So Moses blessed them.

Exodus 39:43

Knock. Knock. Can I come in?" she asked,
peeking her head into my office.

"Uh. . .sure," I said hesitantly.

It was her—"Tammy Talker." Once she entered
your office, you could count on at least a fifteen-
minute distraction.

I'm sure you know Tammy—every office has a
Tammy Talker. You know, the coworker who keeps
you from getting your work done.

While it seems harmless enough, talking at
length with others during the workday is the same
as stealing time from your company. As Christians,
we should go the extra mile when it comes to
integrity. We should make sure that we give an
honest day's work for an honest day's dollar.
We should have the courage to say, "I'd love to talk

with you after work, Tammy, but right now I need to get back to my assignment."

Granted, this response may not make you the most popular gal at work, but sometimes you have to be willing to ruffle a few feathers in order to do the right thing. It is possible to walk in love and integrity at the same time. And, rest assured, God will be pleased with those steps. —MMA

POWER PRAYER
Lord, help me to stand up for what I believe—even if it's not the most popular thing to do. Amen.

Where Am I Going?

Where there is no vision, the people perish.
PROVERBS 29:18 KJV

D o you know any people who took early
retirement and totally lost their drive for
life? I've seen it happen. They lose their vision.
They lose their reason for getting up in the
morning. But you don't have to be of retirement
age to lose your vision. I've seen women of all
ages lose their hope and drive. In fact, I've been
there myself. How about you? There have been
times in my career when I've felt as though I were
drifting on a sea of pointlessness.

No matter where you are in life—right out of
college working your first job or approaching
retirement—you need to have a goal, a dream,

a vision. If you don't, you'll wind up drifting on that same sea of pointlessness, or possibly heading down the river of "I hate my job."

So, do you know God's plan for your life? If not, ask God to show you His vision. Seek His plan, and once you discover it, write it down and keep it before you. Thank Him for that vision every day. Keep the vision close to your heart. Remind yourself of God's plan every time you're asked to do menial tasks at work. Remember, you're on your way to something greater. —MMA

POWER PRAYER

Lord, help me to never lose the vision that You've given me. Amen.

Not Just a Worker Bee

From him the whole body, joined and held together
by every supporting ligament, grows and
builds itself up in love, as each part does its work.

EPHESIANS 4:16

In a meeting that my husband once attended, an executive referred to the attending staff as "worker bees." He said they were not to set the vision, only carry out the project. They weren't to have any ownership, but be mere drones. Of course this fell flat—way flat. On that day, my husband and I both determined that we were more than mere worker bees. And I hope that you make that same determination for yourself.

You may have a position to carry out others' plans, but that doesn't make you a drone who mindlessly works without adding to or taking pride in your job. God has placed gifts and talents in you, some of which you don't even understand yet. He's using you to provide for your family, help others, and be His example. That's not mindless droning. So the next time you feel like a drone, remember: You are more than a worker bee. You are a chosen, called, and gifted child of God! –GM

POWER PRAYER

Thank You, Father, for calling me by name and giving me every gift and talent that I have. I pray that You will help me to diligently use them to bless You and others.

MESSING UP

Neither height nor depth, nor anything else in all
creation, will be able to separate us
from the love of God that is in Christ Jesus our Lord.
ROMANS 8:39

H ave you been to see the boss man yet?" my
friend and coworker asked.

"No, why?" I inquired.

"You had an error in your story. . .it's causing
quite a stir in the newsroom," she shared.

I thought I would vomit. I had written an
entire story, quoting the wrong man. I had lost my
credibility with the readers. I had lost my credibility
with my boss and my coworkers. And I had totally
humiliated myself. It was a very bad day. I felt I had
let everyone down—everyone but God. Not once
did I feel condemned when I brought the dilemma
to Him. In fact, I felt nothing but love. You see,
nothing can separate us from the love of God.

No matter how many times you mess up. No
matter how many things you do wrong.

No matter if your mistake is on the front page of the local newspaper—God still adores you. He's right there with you, ready to help you pick yourself up and start again. So if you've made a gigantic mistake and you need some unconditional love, run to God. He wants to love you today. –MMA

POWER PRAYER
Thank You, Lord, for loving me—even when I make big mistakes. Amen.

I Think I Can Take 'Em

*"You will not have to fight this battle. . .stand firm
and see the deliverance the LORD will give you."*

2 Chronicles 20:17

Do you work with someone who is absolutely impossible? Are there days when you dream about jumping across the conference table and throttling that person? C'mon, be honest. It's tough to get along with every coworker. Some folks are just downright rude. But that doesn't give you the right to return their rudeness.

I used to work with a guy who said crude remarks every time he saw me. One day, he smarted off about my IQ and the size of my chest, and I wanted to deck him. I didn't care if I lost my job over the incident; I was ready to face the consequences. But on my way to his cubicle, the Lord stopped me. I distinctly heard His voice: *"The battle isn't yours."* Oh, but I wanted it to be mine. Still, I knew I had to follow God's leading, so I returned to my office.

A month later, that nasty individual moved—never to be heard from again. God took care of the situation, and I didn't have to lose my job over it. See the battle wasn't mine. It was God's, and He had it under control. Give your battle to God today! —MMA

POWER PRAYER
Lord, I give all of my battles to You. Thanks for taking care of me. Amen.

PICK YOUR BATTLES

A gentle answer turns away wrath,
but a harsh word stirs up anger.

PROVERBS 15:1

One of the greatest lessons I've learned in business is to pick my battles wisely. In stressful environments with intense people, I've seen some people roll with the punches and others explode over every little frustration, causing coworkers to hide under their desks, or at least avoid working with them.

Though there are times when you have to go to battle to correct a wrong, there are other times when peacefully working out a solution with creativity is more effective. By being proactive, instead of constantly looking for a fight, you'll instill trust and cooperation in your coworkers instead of fear and wrath.

Just imagine if every time you approached God, He beat you over the head with your failures. Wouldn't you finally stop approaching Him or live in fear of His reaction? Yes, He still corrects you, and His Holy Spirit still convicts you for wrongdoing, but you can be at peace, knowing that He only wants what's best for you. —GM

POWER PRAYER

Lord, thank You for my coworkers. I pray for Your blessings on them and ask that You help me to work well with them.

If You Need Me,
I'll Be under My Desk
with Bonbons

"Don't be afraid," the prophet answered.
"Those who are with us are
more than those who are with them."

2 Kings 6:16

Ever felt like you were all alone in your company? Ever felt so outnumbered by your adversaries that you wanted to crawl under your desk and hide? We've all been there, and it's not an easy place to be.

But isn't it comforting to know that we don't have to go it alone? God says He will never leave us nor forsake us.

Need some more convincing? Read about Elisha in 2 Kings, chapter 6. The king of Aram was angry with Elisha and came after him. When Elisha and his servant awoke the next morning, the servant saw the enemy's army with horses and chariots surrounding the city. The servant was scared and asked, "What shall we do?" Elisha assured him, "Those who are with us are more than those who are with them." Then Elisha prayed for the servant's eyes to be opened so he could see the real situation—the hills full of horses and chariots of fire all around them. God had the situation under control.

Even though you may feel alone today, just know that God has an army working for you. Ask God to help you see your situation through His eyes. And rejoice in your impending victory.
—MMA

POWER PRAYER
Thank You, Lord, for protecting me from my enemies. Amen.

I Think I Can

I can do everything through him who gives me strength.
PHILIPPIANS 4:13

Remember the Little Golden Book about the little engine that could? You know the story. He tries really hard—against many odds—chugging along and puffing, "I think I can, I think I can" until he proves everyone wrong and reaches his goal. I've always loved that little book. You know why? Because it's packed with powerful teaching. If we can keep a can-do attitude, we can achieve many things.

My eleven-year-old daughter, Abby, is a great gymnast. In fact, she is a member of a competitive gymnastics team. When Abby is preparing for her tumbling pass, I can always tell if she's going to do well just by the look on her face. If she approaches the mat with a can-do facial expression, I know she's going to nail it. But if she shows fear on her face, I know she's not going to give her best performance. It's all in the attitude.

Maybe you have a goal that seems impossible to reach—sort of like the little engine that could. Maybe your boss has put you in charge of something that seems impossible. Well, God says that you can do all things through Him, so go for it! Keep a can-do attitude, and watch your dreams become a reality! —MMA

POWER PRAYER
Lord, help me to have a can-do attitude. Amen.

These Changes
Are Making Me Crazy

Jesus Christ is the same yesterday and today and forever.
HEBREWS 13:8

Have you ever heard the song "Changes" by Three Doors Down? The chorus goes: "Now I'm going through changes, changes. God, I feel so frustrated lately. When I get suffocated, save me. Now I'm going through changes, changes. I'm running, shaking. Bound and breaking. I hope I make it through all these changes."

Yep, there have been times in my career when that song could've been my anthem. Ever been there? When companies go through "changes," many times they incorporate new policies, new management, and extreme restructuring. I worked for a magazine that restructured three times in three years! I always joked, "If I'm let go over the weekend, please call me so I can bring in a box for my belongings on Monday." But in reality, things were almost that crazy!

When change smacks you in the face, there's only one thing to do—run to God. No matter what kind of craziness is going on where you work, you can rest in this truth—God never changes. His Word says that He is the same—yesterday, today, and forever. So place your future in His hands. It's a good place to be! –MMA

POWER PRAYER
Lord, I am so frustrated with the changes at work. Please help me to look past the circumstances. I put my future in Your hands. Amen.

The Best Kind of Thinking

As charcoal to embers and as wood to fire,
so is a quarrelsome man for kindling strife.

PROVERBS 26:21

One of my managers, JoAnn, was a great team builder. She could rally a group of people to work harder and longer than ever. When challenges came her way, she wasn't always happy about it, but she always gave people the benefit of the doubt. Through experience she'd learned that workers sometimes faced unusual challenges, and her example taught me a valuable lesson: Think the best of others.

Over the years, I've tried to keep this lesson at the forefront of my mind. Of course, there will be those few difficult, incompetent workers,

but usually people want to be good at their jobs. So though you may have to deal with a few bad apples, wouldn't you rather err on the side of thinking the best of someone who didn't deserve it than the other way around?

God wants you to be a peacemaker wherever you go. He wants you to stand out as someone who avoids strife and builds others up. As you do, you'll continue to be a light that others will trust and follow. —GM

POWER PRAYER

Lord, help me to see the best in others. Help me to be a peacemaker and build others up so that I can be a light for You in everything I do.

Stars and Starfish

"For the battle is the LORD's."
1 Samuel 17:47

When I was in seventh-grade biology, our class was divided into pairs and asked to dissect a starfish. Yuck! I had quite a weak stomach, and I knew I'd hurl if I had to touch that stinky starfish. However, I was a fast note taker and a pretty good typist. So my partner and I agreed to work with our strengths—he did the gross stuff, and I did the rest. Our teamwork paid off! We received an A.

If only every task worked out so well in the real world.

Have you ever been paired up with someone in your company who simply wouldn't do any work? It's the worst! You want to expose your lazy partner, but you're afraid to appear like less than a team player. It's a difficult, yet common, situation.

Maybe you're in that predicament today. If so, hang in there. Just remember that even if your boss never knows how much work you've done (and how little your partner has produced), God knows. Don't become bitter. Simply continue doing your best work. God will cause your actions (and your partner's inaction) to get noticed by those in authority. Soon, you'll be a star and your partner will be a stinky starfish. —MMA

POWER PRAYER
Lord, help me to keep a right attitude even in bad situations. Amen.

ROUND AND ROUND IT GOES

The words of a gossip are like choice morsels;
they go down to a man's inmost parts.

PROVERBS 26:22

few years ago, my company underwent a
restructure. During that time, several
important people were reassigned or dismissed.
It was a difficult time for everyone. But even
worse than what happened was listening to the
rumor mill churn. Every day there were more and
more theories tossed around about who was
leaving and how jobs were going to be reorganized.
Just listening to the churning caused people to
become anxious—regardless of whether the
rumors were true or not.

I have a friend who is brilliant at avoiding the
rumor mill. She will change the subject or quietly

walk away from conversations. I'll admit that I strive to be more like her 100 percent of the time. Unfortunately, sometimes I fail.

Imagine if everyone determined to avoid the rumor mill, making the decision to change the subject or walk away from hurtful conversations. Perhaps the next helpless victim would be saved, and there'd be less anxiety in the workplace. You never know—it could just be the first step in winning your office for Jesus. —GM

POWER PRAYER

Lord, please help me to stand strong against the office rumor mill so that I don't hurt others. Let me be a part of the rumor mill solution.

GETTING ZINGED

"Bless those who curse you,
pray for those who mistreat you."
LUKE 6:28

Let's be honest; we've all been zinged. You know, those comments that are said so sweetly that it isn't until you walk away that you realize you were insulted, like, "I *love* your hair; it looks like something from the forties." Yeah, I loved hearing that one.

As an individual who is blessed to breathe air, you're sure to have received a zinger. And as women, we've been blessed with long memories that allow us to relive those comments over and over again.

When the zingers come—and they *will* come—you have two choices. You can respond emotionally, leaving godly grace at the door, or you can respond in love—either by remaining silent or by *gently* responding to the comment. The choice is yours.

However, if you're listening to the Holy Spirit, you know that He won't let you get away with responding with a verbal assault. No, it's much better to respond in love. And the next time you see the "zingee," follow the advice found in Luke 6:28, and pray for God's blessing in her life. As you do, God promises that "your reward will be great" (Luke 6:35), and you will become more and more like Him. –GM

POWER PRAYER
Lord, I ask that You help me to be an example of Your love and grace in everything I do.

BAD DAYS

But David encouraged himself in the LORD his God.

1 SAMUEL 30:6 KJV

I want you to stop and think about the very worst day you've ever spent on the job. Okay, have you got a visual? Did you just want to throw your hands into the air and quit on that day? Did you feel like God had forsaken you? Did you want to head for a tropical island and never return? I think we've all been there. Even David had some bad days "on the job."

He was doing exactly what God had told him to do, fighting battles for God. But when he and his men returned from war on this particular day, they found their city had been burned and all of their wives and children had been taken. You talk about a bad day on the job! And to make matters worse, all of David's men turned on him and plotted together to stone him. Things looked pretty bleak, but David didn't crawl into a hole and curse God. No, instead the Bible says that David encouraged himself in the Lord. And you know what? It wasn't long before that entire situation turned around in David's favor.

So no matter how bad it may get at work, follow David's example. Encourage yourself in the Lord, and watch your situation turn around! —MMA

POWER PRAYER
Thank You, Lord, for Your never-ending faithfulness! Amen.

LOOKING OUT
FOR NUMBER ONE

At that time the disciples came to Jesus and asked,
"Who is the greatest in the kingdom of heaven?"
He called a little child and had him stand among them.
And he said: ". . .Whoever humbles himself like
this child is the greatest in the kingdom of heaven."

MATTHEW 18:1–4

I find this passage really interesting. Here the disciples were walking with Jesus, and they were more concerned about themselves than the job at hand. I'm sure Jesus' response really took them aback. He gently held up a child as a standard of faith and humility. Though it sounds simple, I'm sure if I had been standing there, I would have been tempted to ask, "Yeah, but what are the three steps to being number one?"

I can be a bit stubborn sometimes.

So how can you be the greatest you can be with God? Well, if you love and serve Him with

childlike faith and humility, you already are.
Take comfort in that and continue to be faithful
to Him. Loving Him with your whole heart will
bring you more satisfaction than any other
position you'll ever hold. —GM

MR. GRUMPY

A cheerful look brings joy to the heart.
PROVERBS 15:30

He was always grumpy. He hated his marriage. He hated his job. He hated his life. And from what I could tell, he hated everyone in the office. Call me crazy, but it became my mission to get a grin out of this guy. However, he made it very difficult. He grouched and grumbled on a daily basis. Once I offered to get Mr. Grumpy a soft drink since I was on my way back to the lunchroom, and he grumbled, "Are you trying to kill me? Do you know what's in that junk?"

This guy was a real piece of work. I never made much progress with this grumpy old guy, but I did manage to muster a smile or two over the years. When I moved to take another job, he even gave me a hug at my going-away luncheon! The entire office staff gasped, sure he was lunging toward me to swing at me, not hug me.

You know, there are grumpy people at every workplace—people who'd rather scowl than smile. But don't let their grumpiness steal your joy. Instead, share your joy with them! Go out of your way to be nice to them. Just think. . .you may be the only Christian in their lives. —MMA

POWER PRAYER
Lord, fill me with Your joy so that I might share it with others. Amen.

Driven to Succeed

"Don't panic. I'm with you. There's no need to fear
for I'm your God. I'll give you strength. I'll help you.
I'll hold you steady, keep a firm grip on you."
ISAIAH 41:10 MSG

I once sat in a seminar where a successful female executive admitted that the catalyst that drove her to succeed was a fear of failure. She owned several businesses, including a consulting firm and two employment agencies. Personally, she had faced a divorce, remarriage, stepparenting, and a substance-abuse problem. While I admired her success, it saddened me that she'd faced it alone.

As a Christian, you have such an advantage in Jesus. You are never alone. I know that when fear has gripped me, I haven't had my eyes focused on Jesus. Instead, I've tried to do everything in my own strength. As women, we often fall into doing things in our own strength. We try to accomplish so much—personally and professionally—that it's easy to forget that we don't have to carry everything ourselves. Jesus is there to help carry our burdens and overcome our fears. Trust Jesus to help you increase your faith and destroy your fear through His Word. –GM

POWER PRAYER

Lord, I am struggling with a fear that's making it difficult for me to make the decisions I need to make. I trust that through Your Word my faith and peace will increase.

On Your Way
to the Corner Office

A heart at peace gives life to the body,
but envy rots the bones.

PROVERBS 14:30

Staring at the inside of my green cubicle, I wondered if God even knew that I existed. It seemed everyone around me was moving up in the company, but not me. No matter how hard I worked, no one seemed to notice or care. Ever been there?

It's an unpleasant place to be. That "what about me?" mentality eventually leads to jealousy, envy, bitterness, and hopelessness. So if you're dwelling in that "what about me?" land, head for the border!

If you can't be happy for your coworker when she finally gets promoted, God will never be able to bless you with your dream job. If you can't celebrate with your boss when he is awarded a Caribbean cruise for a job well done, God will never be able to bless you with company perks.

In the midst of everybody else's dreams coming true, we have to keep our hearts right. If we don't, we'll never get to walk in ours. Keep your eyes on God, and He will make your dreams come true, too. Don't worry when you see others getting blessed. He has more than enough blessings to go around. —MMA

POWER PRAYER

Lord, help me to be happy when my coworkers realize their dreams because I know my dreams will also come true. Amen.

An Open Line

*Then Jesus told his disciples a parable to show
them that they should always pray and not give up.*

LUKE 18:1

Recently I attended a meeting with a woman
who, in the midst of our meeting, received a
phone call. Then a few minutes later, while she
was still on the phone, she received another call
on her cell phone. Over the next five minutes,
I watched as she juggled both calls at once—
one phone on each ear—never breaking her stride.

As Christians, we need to have two receivers
open, too—one to those around us and the other
to God. In Luke 18, Jesus told the disciples to
"always pray." As eager as you may be to get that
helpful phone call at work with just the right

information, as a child of God, you should be just as eager to get direction and information from God. Some people assume that if you're not in a certain place or praying in a certain way, it doesn't count. But actually, God never hangs up the spiritual phone; He's always on the line, hoping that you'll have your receiver pressed against your ear.

As you go through your day, keep your prayer line open, becoming even more in tune with Him. —GM

WHERE'D THAT WRENCH
COME FROM?

"I command you—be strong and courageous!
Do not be afraid or discouraged.
For the LORD your God is with you wherever you go."
JOSHUA 1:9 NLT

W e need to stop that project to make a
change," my manager called as she rushed
by my door. "Grab your files and come to my
office." Of course, it was five o'clock and I had an

appointment, but none of that mattered because a wrench—an unexpected change—had occurred.

After a few days of going through the wrench cycle—disbelief, frustration, and full-blown anger with a dash of self-pity—I picked myself up and started again. Welcome to the business world! I would love for projects to run smoothly from beginning to end, but wrenches happen to the best-laid plans.

If you've been thrown a wrench, don't get discouraged. Changes and disappointments are a part of working with people, but you can rise above them. Stay humble and keep a sense of humor. Focus on God, and then take a deep breath and move forward. When the project is completed, you'll have a sense of satisfaction, and in time, you won't even remember the wrenches. You'll only remember the success. –GM

POWER PRAYER

Lord, help me to have strength and courage when wrenches come my way and to trust You to direct me every day.

Employee of the Month

"Be still, and know that I am God."

PSALM 46:10

Don't you hate it when a coworker takes credit for something that you accomplished? It's even worse when a supervisor takes credit for your work. Ever been there?

I once sat in a meeting and listened to my boss read an idea that I'd submitted without ever revealing the source of that idea. When the "big bosses" raved over my idea, my boss was a hero, and I was furious. I couldn't believe that another human being, especially someone I had trusted, could be so deceitful.

I had two choices: Let the big man in the company know about my supervisor's behavior, or let it go and walk away. My flesh wanted to shout from the rooftops that the idea had been mine—all mine. But the Holy Spirit wouldn't let me. Instead, I kept hearing that verse, "Be still, and know that I am God." So that's the direction I took, and God honored my obedience. Shortly thereafter, I was named employee of the month!

God will cause your ideas to rise to the top. He will make sure that your bosses know you are an asset to the company. After all, He is actually in charge, and He adores you! –MMA

POWER PRAYER
Lord, I put my career in Your hands. Thank You for bringing my good work to the attention of the powers that be. Amen.

Juicy Fruits

A gossip betrays a confidence;
so avoid a man who talks too much.

PROVERBS 20:19

S o do you have anything juicy to tell me?" my
coworker asked.

I smiled nervously and answered, "No, but I
do have some Juicy Fruit gum in my purse."

She rolled her eyes and smiled, hurrying to
her desk. I was glad. I had avoided yet another
gossip session with a coworker. Since my sister
was higher up in the company than I was, she was
privileged to information that others were not.
Of course, my sister shared some information
with me—tidbits that I had promised not to repeat.
My coworkers knew this and pumped me for
"juicy tidbits" every chance they got.

And to be honest, it was a struggle. I loved
being "in the know." But I knew in my heart that I
couldn't tell anything that my sister had shared
with me in confidence. If I did, I'd be letting her
down, and even worse, I'd be letting God down.
So I tried my best to avoid those situations.

Maybe you're in an office where gossiping is a problem. If you tend to join in the "gossip fests," ask God to help you in this area. Let your words reflect those of the Father. Those are the only words worth sharing. —MMA

POWER PRAYER
Lord, help me to speak only the things You would have me say. Amen.

Readjusting the Compass

The steps of a good man are ordered by the LORD:
and he delighteth in his way.

PSALM 37:23 KJV

My friends will sometimes ask me, "Are you still working as much, or are you taking time off to relax?" I usually just laugh and shrug because to me, it's just life as usual. I'm like most women; I work, play, socialize, and worship—sometimes all at the same time.

But every so often, I have to readjust my schedule. It's as though the needle on my internal compass has to be readjusted to point north again. I take a deep breath, put aside some time for myself, and get before the Lord for a heart-to-heart. This isn't a quick five-minute appointment.

It's a several-day journey where I reevaluate my priorities and ask God to nix anything that isn't necessary to help me refocus.

If you're feeling like you're low on energy and have no time for yourself, take time to have a heart-to-heart with God. Ask Him to readjust your compass and show you where to focus your energies. With a renewed sense of purpose and direction, you'll have the energy to do what you really need to be doing. —GM

POWER PRAYER

Lord, I am so busy that I can't even decipher what things on my to-do list are truly necessary. Help me to reprioritize and focus on what You want me to do.

GIVE THEM YOUR DUE

The entire law is summed up in a single command:
"Love your neighbor as yourself."

GALATIANS 5:14

D o you feel like you're always going the extra mile and being taken advantage of? I imagine Abraham felt the same way when Lot chose the best piece of land. Remember that story?

Abraham followed God's leading and gathered all his family, traveling for months before finally arriving in the new land. But after being there only a short while, they discovered there wasn't enough land and water to support all the people and flocks. So Abraham told Lot, "We're going to have to separate. Choose whichever piece of land you want, and I'll take whatever is left over." Lot looked around and chose the beautiful green, lush valley, leaving Abraham an old dry field.

Don't you imagine that Abraham felt used and unappreciated? But that's not where the story ends. See, Abraham climbed the highest mountain and looked in every direction. Then God said, "As far as you can see, I'll give it all to you." That's the kind of God we serve.

When you're good to people, God will make sure you come out on top. God sees you preferring other people. Nothing that you do goes unnoticed by Almighty God. Honor others and God will honor you. —MMA

POWER PRAYER
Lord, help me to treat others as You would have me to do. Amen.

Follow the Leader

*"Anyone who intends to come with me has to let me lead.
You're not in the driver's seat; I am."*

MATTHEW 16:24 MSG

The workplace is an interesting and comical place to play follow the leader. I once had a beautiful, talented boss who was successful in many areas. She was a visionary at work and a wonder-woman wife and mother. Many wanted to be like her. If she changed her hairstyle, women changed theirs, too. If she wore certain brand-name clothes, others followed. People followed her diets, exercise regimens, and even changed to use her OB/GYN doctor. Because obviously, hers was better, right?

There will always be talented people you admire. They'll teach you how to succeed, and it would be foolish not to learn from them; but ultimately Jesus is the best role model you could ever have. His is the greatest example of love, compassion, leadership, hard work, and humility. His life is the one you want to emulate. So play follow the leader with Jesus, allowing His ways to become your ways. Put Him in the driver's seat of your life, realizing that He is your ultimate role model. As you do, you'll become more and more like Him. –GM

POWER PRAYER

Lord, thank You for being in the driver's seat in my life. I follow You first and pray that Your ways become my ways.

TERRITORIAL STANDOFFS

A gentle answer turns away wrath,
but a harsh word stirs up anger.

PROVERBS 15:1

Once as a new hire, I found myself facing off with a veteran worker. At the time, I couldn't figure out what I had done to offend her, but it was apparent that my very presence was an irritation. Of course, I now realize that many of her responsibilities were shifted over to me. Obviously, there was a lot more going on with her than what I knew.

When you become the object of someone's scorn for no apparent reason, it probably has nothing to do with you personally. You're simply the catalyst. Anger is a difficult emotion to navigate, whether it belongs to someone in the workplace, home, or even the dry cleaner's. God's Word instructs us to have a kind word for those who are angry, which unfortunately is a constant state of being for some.

If you're confronted with an angry person, pray for wisdom for the situation. Make the decision not to match her actions. Instead, remain calm, kind, and objective. By doing this, you may not see an immediate change in her demeanor, but you'll be a witness—possibly the only witness—of kindness in her life. –GM

POWER PRAYER
Dear Lord, thank You for helping me to be kind to others, even when they're angry. Help me to be a witness for You today.

A Cubicle by the Window

*Do not think of yourself more highly
than you ought, but rather think of yourself
with sober judgment, in accordance
with the measure of faith God has given you.*

Romans 12:3

Isn't it funny how small things can determine
someone's importance? Some revere those who
are born to a certain family. Others honor those
who have certain possessions. And in office society,

corner offices or cubicles by the window are coveted. They're given to the chosen, honored few.

Everyone wants to be respected. But if you already have respect and honor, don't forget that there was a time when you didn't have the corner office or window view. Once, you were the one desperately trying to prove yourself to the office veterans.

When it comes to respecting others, it's best to follow God's example. He never looks down on you because of what you do or don't have. Instead, He looks at your heart. And even when you were covered with ugly ungodliness, He sent His Son to die for you.

As you go through your day, don't forget to show compassion and kindness for those around you. Value others for the people God made them to be. After all, that's what's truly important. —GM

POWER PRAYER

Thank You, Lord, for helping me to value others.
Show me how to be an example of Your compassion
and kindness to them.

WILL THIS STORM EVER END?

*But God remembered Noah and all the wild animals
and the livestock that were with him in the ark, and he
sent a wind over the earth, and the waters receded.*

GENESIS 8:1

Can you imagine being on a boat with a
bunch of smelly animals for 150 days?
(Remind you of your workplace?) Well. . .Noah
and his family did just that. Some people think
they only had to survive on that boat for 40 days
and 40 nights, but the Bible says it *rained* for 40
days and 40 nights, but it took 150 days for the
water to go down enough for Noah and the gang
to exit the boat.

I'm sure there were days when Noah and his
family wished they hadn't been chosen for the ark

assignment. But Noah knew God, and he believed that God would deliver them—no matter how many days he looked outside and saw nothing but water. For almost seven months, the Lord caused the wind to blow and push back the floodwaters. God was working behind the scenes the whole time.

Maybe you feel like you're on a big boat, floating on a sea of insecurities right now. You may not be able to see a change today, but just trust in Him. God hasn't forgotten you. In fact, your miracle may blow in on the very next breeze. —MMA

POWER PRAYER
Lord, help me to trust You more. Amen.

Bring Your Own Paper Clips

Cast your cares on the LORD and he will sustain you.

PSALM 55:22

Ever felt persecuted at work? Ever felt like everyone else was treated better than you? Once when I was working as a writer for a magazine, I requested a box of paper clips on the office order sheet. I didn't ask for a display phone, which all of the other writers had. (My phone was so old, it didn't ring. It sort of moaned!) No, all I requested was a box of paper clips. I never dreamed my request would be denied.

That afternoon, my supervisor poked her head into my office and said, "You'll need to bring paper clips from home. We're only purchasing the absolutely necessary items." I could not believe it! I thought, *Do you mean I work my guts out for this company, and I'm not even worth a thirty-nine-cent box of paper clips?* Then, I started noticing how many other "office items" my cowriters had that

I did not have. The more I made mental notes about my "have-not" situation, the worse I felt and the worse I acted.

Ever been there? Maybe you are getting the short end of the stick in your workplace, but don't dwell on it. Give your situation to Him. God cares about everything that affects you—even a paper clip shortage! –MMA

POWER PRAYER

Lord, help me to keep my heart right in the midst of this mistreatment. Amen.

Have Mercy on Me

*"Shouldn't you have had mercy
on your fellow servant just as I had on you?"*
MATTHEW 18:33

Have you ever made a big mistake at work? Not a little oops, but a full-blown "oh-no" kind of mistake? I have. Once in the midst of developing a direct-mail piece, I left off a crucial piece of information, a last-minute, special guest appearance at an international convention. After my boss's boss called to ask why it wasn't on the final piece, I dove into my notes only to discover that I had received the information. I swallowed my pride and admitted my mistake. Oh, that was a painful phone call. She could have yelled at me, threatened me, fired me, or placed a letter of reprimand in my

personnel file. But, amazingly, she was merciful. She began brainstorming about other ways to advertise the guest appearance. Disaster averted.

If you've ever received mercy, then you can understand the parable of the unmerciful servant (Matthew 18:21–35). You know how thankful you are to receive mercy and how important it is to extend it to others. It's part of the favor and grace that God, through His Son Jesus, showed to you and a reflection of the favor and grace that you should show to others. –GM

POWER PRAYER
Dear heavenly Father, thank You for Your mercy, grace, and forgiveness. Help me to show that same grace to others.

SHE IS YOU!

She considers a field and buys it; out of her earnings she plants a vineyard. She sets about her work vigorously. . . . She sees that her trading is profitable.

PROVERBS 31:16—18

Have you ever read Proverbs 31? I mean, really read it in light of your life? So often people visualize a truly godly woman as a quiet little church mouse, but if you read Proverbs 31, you'll see that she is really a savvy businesswoman. She is frugal, business-minded, and hardworking, much like the modern working woman. She cares for her family, buys land, expands her crops, and gets good deals.

Sound familiar? Sure it does.

She's you as you balance your career and family. She's you when you work to make the best sales and meet your employer's goals, while serving the Lord with your whole heart.

Don't believe that because you work outside of the home, you will never attain the godly, Proverbs 31 woman's image. The truth is that the gifts and talents you have are God-given, and as you use them, you are honoring Him, which is the true vision of the Proverbs 31 woman. –GM

POWER PRAYER

Dear Father, thank You for providing for me and for using me to accomplish Your will in my family's lives and in mine. I pray that I will glorify You in all I do.

THE DREAM LIST

Write the vision, and make it plain upon tables,
that he may run that readeth it.

HABAKKUK 2:2 KJV

Years ago, I made a list of things I wanted to do in my lifetime. It included things like sailing around the world, attending the Olympics, going on a cruise, and traveling Europe by train with my husband. I haven't accomplished all of them, and some I no longer have an interest in doing, like skydiving or hang gliding. (Those urges passed with the big hair of the 1980s.) Still, it's fun to review the list and see how many I've accomplished, which ones I no longer want to do, and others that are yet to be done. And of course, there are always new ones to add.

Writing down a vision—whether personal or professional—is a great way to keep your dreams in front of you. And as time passes, it's a great encouragement. During those times when you feel like you're going nowhere, your list can remind you of all that you've accomplished. Then you can thank God for giving you the desires of your heart, because He is the Author and Finisher of your life. –GM

POWER PRAYER
Lord, thank You for giving me dreams and visions. I dedicate them and my life to You.

Guess What I Learned
at the Watercooler?

Do not let any unwholesome talk
come out of your mouths, but only what is helpful for
building others up according to their needs,
that it may benefit those who listen.

EPHESIANS 4:29

H e is such a moron," your coworker whispers
over lunch.

"No kidding. How did he get to be boss?" your
other friend chimes in. "He is so incompetent.
And is he ever a lousy dresser! What is with that
tie today?"

"I know. He is such a loser!" you add, forming
the L sign with your right hand.

Ahh. . .lunchtime chatter. It's all harmless,
right? Well, not exactly. According to Ephesians
4:29, we aren't supposed to let *any* unwholesome
talk come out of our mouths.

Take your mother's advice: If you can't say something nice, don't say anything at all. Remember, your words are powerful. They can be building blocks or wrecking balls, so use them wisely. Don't bad-mouth your boss with your coworkers. Instead, find positive comments and observations to make. Be the positive force in your office.

This will take practice. You may have to bite your tongue really hard to keep from participating in the next boss-bashing session, but God will help you. Ask the Holy Spirit to keep a watch over your words. He will. And soon your words will create a better work environment. —MMA

POWER PRAYER
Lord, help me to only speak words that build up, not tear down. Amen.

No-Man's-Land

I will say of the LORD, "He is my refuge
and my fortress, my God, in whom I trust."

PSALM 91:2

Once upon a time, I worked with two managers who feuded constantly. I don't know what started the feuding, but I do know that it made for a *challenging* work environment. It was a no-man's-land, a place where no one wins and even the simplest tasks become major battles.

Unfortunately, this isn't unusual. Even in the Bible, Jonathan lived in a no-man's-land between his father, Saul, and his blood brother, David. His father wanted to kill David while David raced around the countryside trying to understand why (1 Samuel 20). Fortunately, God's plan won out.

In the same way, God has a plan for you. It doesn't mean that you won't face uncomfortable situations, but it does mean that God can give you the grace to handle them. He may lead you to another position or direct you to be an example of peaceful professionalism. Regardless, keep praying. Don't get dragged into office gossip. Instead, focus on your work and pray. More than any anger, fear, or distrust, your prayers will be the real force. –GM

POWER PRAYER

Lord, You know the situation even better than I do. I pray that You'll show me how to pray for the people involved and be an example of peaceful professionalism.

TWISTED WORDS

"For God so loved the world
that he gave his one and only Son."
JOHN 3:16

I once oversaw a project that turned out to be a disappointment. Because I understood the challenges with it, I had taken a *c'est la vie* approach to the results. When I showed it to a coworker who had worked on it, I explained what had happened. She wasn't so understanding and decided to confront a manager in another department about it. During her rampage, she told the manager that I was "very upset." As you can imagine, things escalated and it took two meetings and several weeks to repair the damage that she'd created—all because she'd twisted my words.

It got me thinking that sometimes we do this to God, too. We take His Word out of context. Instead of accepting that He loves us just as we are, we think: *If only I change this or do that, then God will love me.* The truth is that God accepts us just the way we are. He may want to perfect something in our lives, but He still loves us—wholly and without reservation. So the next time you start to view yourself differently than God's Word says, remind yourself what His words *say*—truthfully and untwisted. –GM

POWER PRAYER
Thank You, Lord, for loving me just as I am. I will look to Your Word for the truth about who I am in Your eyes.

DREAMS CAN BE REAL,
CAN'T THEY?

*"If you believe, you will
receive whatever you ask for in prayer."*
MATTHEW 21:22

I have a friend whose actual job is to go into people's homes and organize them from top to bottom. I can't even imagine doing that. I mean, I have so many "junk drawers" in my house, it takes me thirty minutes to locate the scissors each time I need them. Can I have an "amen"? Obviously, organization is not one of my gifts.

I have another friend who teaches twenty-five kindergarteners for a living. Yes, she is a wonderful teacher. While I adore children, I knew I wasn't called to be a teacher after substitute teaching for a brief stint. Who knew 8 a.m. to 3 p.m. could last so long?

But you know what is so cool? Both of my friends absolutely love what they do, and they are awesome at their individual callings. They are truly walking in their professional dreams.

That's what I love about our heavenly Father. He gives each of us unique dreams, and then He equips us to accomplish those dreams if we'll only believe. It gives Him great joy to see us pursuing the ambitions He has placed within us. So hang in there! God can't wait to see you walking in your dream. –MMA

POWER PRAYER

Lord, thank You for placing unique dreams in my heart. Amen.

POWERFUL WORDS

The tongue that brings healing is a tree of life,
but a deceitful tongue crushes the spirit.
PROVERBS 15:4

Have you ever considered how powerful your words are? I can remember things that people have said to me—both positive and negative—that still resonate in my mind. I've been called a creative problem solver, but then I've also been told that I'm a pushover. The good is nice to hear, but the bad is hard to swallow. I have to consciously remind myself not to see myself that way.

Why? Because words are powerful. They can build up or tear down; it's that simple. The amazing thing to realize is that our words can have a similar power over other people. What we say can build

them up or tear them down, affecting how they view themselves.

As an ambassador of Christ, you're in a powerful position where it is necessary to build others up, being a positive influence in their lives instead of a destructive force. You have that power and responsibility. So today, as you interact with coworkers, some of whom may grate on your nerves, determine to build them up. You never know—your kind words may be the only ones they hear. –GM

POWER PRAYER
Lord, as an ambassador for You, help me to bring healing and encouragement to others today.

The Only Change I Want
Is from the Snack Machine

*"Be strong and courageous. . .for the LORD
your God goes with you;
he will never leave you nor forsake you."*

DEUTERONOMY 31:6

As I watched the moving truck pull away,
a pang of fear shot through my body.
This pang was followed by waves of questions:
*Are we doing the right thing? How will we survive in
a big city? Is this fair to our children? Will I even like
my new job?*

I had married my high school sweetheart.
After graduating from college, we had settled into
nice, comfy jobs in our hometown. My parents
even lived next door to us. It was the perfect
setup. We were sure we'd live and die in Bedford,
Indiana. So when I was offered a tremendous
magazine writing job in Fort Worth, Texas, we were
unsure of what to do. After much prayer, we felt
God calling us west.

Talk about a big change! Even though I knew we were in the center of God's will, I worried. But God was with us every step of the way, reassuring us of our decision. There are days that I still get homesick, but I'm never alone. If you're facing some major changes today—cross-country moves or job transfers—you don't have to go it alone, either. God will go with you. –MMA

POWER PRAYER
Lord, I am afraid of change. Help me to face these changes with joy and strength. I love You. Amen.

LIGHTEN UP

For God hath not given us the spirit of fear;
but of power, and of love, and of a sound mind.

2 TIMOTHY 1:7 KJV

A re you way too hard on yourself? If you are, you're not alone. As working women, we expect a lot out of ourselves. We have to if we want to stay in the game, right? But many times we put such unrealistic expectations on ourselves that we're in a constant state of panic—afraid of failure.

That's no way to live, sister. The Bible says that we have not been given a spirit of fear but of power, love, and a sound mind. Yet we go around biting our freshly manicured fingernails, worrying about a missed opportunity or a less-than-stellar job review. Take a deep breath and stop worrying.

Of course, we're going to drop the ball once in a while. But don't beat yourself up. Accept your mistakes, learn from them, and move on.

Don't waste your time worrying (which is a sneaky form of fear) about what could've, should've, or might've been. God wants you to live free from fear. Remember, the Word also says that when we are weak, He is strong. That means, even when you miss it, God has got your back! —MMA

POWER PRAYER

Lord, I give all of my fears to You today. Help me to stop setting unrealistic goals. I only want what You want for me. Amen.

It's My Office
and I'll Cry If I Want To

As far as the east is from the west,
so far has he removed our transgressions from us.

PSALM 103:12

When I get mad, I cry. Are you like that, too? It's just as well, really, because my tears keep me from saying too many things I'd later regret. Why? Because it's hard to talk when you're blubbering like an idiot.

However, I've been known to say a few ugly remarks between sobs. Sure, I was sorry later, but I couldn't retrieve my words. Have you ever been there? Have you ever wished you could hit the rewind button and retract the words you just screamed at your boss? Oh, yeah. . .we've all been there.

Well, I've got good news. Even though you can't take back the words you yelled at your boss, you can apologize to him or her, and pray for God's intervention on your behalf. And here's more good news: You *can* hit the rewind button with God. Once you ask for forgiveness, God doesn't remember your harsh, sinful comments anymore. He totally erases them from His memory. The Word says He removes our transgressions "as far as the east is from the west," and that's a good little piece, as they say in Texas. So dry your eyes. God isn't mad at you. –MMA

POWER PRAYER

Thank You, Lord, for loving me—no matter what.
Help me to walk in Your love. Amen.

A CHANGE OF ATTITUDE

"God is with you in everything you do."
GENESIS 21:22

I absolutely loved my boss. He was gentle. He was kind. He was brilliant. And he was quick to offer assistance. Basically, he was the perfect boss. So when I changed jobs and encountered the exact opposite of my beloved former boss, I panicked. Everything I had respected about my former boss—

his dedication to the craft, his backbone, his humor, his willingness to share his gift, his humility— were all lost on my new boss.

I was just about to call my former boss and go crawling back with my tail between my legs, begging for my old position, when I remembered a verse I'd learned in Bible school twenty years before. "God is with you in everything you do." The more I thought about it, the more encouraged I became. I realized that even though I no longer had the perfect boss, I still had God. And He promised to work alongside me in everything I did. That was good enough for me.

See, my situation didn't change for the better, but my attitude did. And that made all the difference. If you're unhappy in your job, change your attitude. Praise God that you have a job, and remember that He is with you today and always. –MMA

POWER PRAYER
Thank You, Lord, for my job. Please change my attitude so that I might honor You in my work. Amen.

Enjoying the Favor of God and Man

When Aaron and all the Israelites saw Moses,
his face was radiant.

Exodus 34:30

Have you ever been around someone who actually glows? You can't really explain it, but that coworker simply beams. He or she outshines everyone else in the office. Yeah, we all know someone who walks in absolute favor. Usually, those folks are the ones who rise to the top with great ease. You know why? They are filled with God's presence! They glow with the glory of the Lord. That's why they outshine everyone else. That's why they are so attractive to others. That's why everyone is open to their ideas. That's why they are promoted when others are being let go.

Did you know after Moses had spent time with God, he would have to wear a veil over his face because he glowed too brightly for the Israelites to behold him? See, if you spend time with God—reading your Bible and talking to Him and praising Him—you will begin to glow, too! You'll start changing from the inside out. It'll be just like that *Extreme Makeover* show on TV, but you'll be extremely made over on the inside, which will overflow to your outside.

Why not spend some time with God today and begin your Master Makeover? You glow, girl!
—MMA

POWER PRAYER
Lord, fill me with more of You that I might radiate Your love. Amen.

Pardon Me,
May I Use You as a Rung?

Love. . .is not self-seeking.

1 Corinthians 13:4–5

Love is not self-seeking. Well, that's a tough one to live in today's workplace, isn't it? I mean, if you don't look out for number one, nobody else will, right? The world would have you think that you have to push and claw your way to the top—even at the expense of others. But that's not God's way of doing things. God wants to promote you in His way—in His time.

You don't have to "play the game" to climb the corporate ladder. You don't have to step on others to get ahead. You can rest in God, knowing that He has a good plan for your life.

Maybe you've been hurt by a coworker. Maybe someone that you trusted in your company betrayed you to gain placement in the company. It happens, but don't let that situation get you off track. Continue to walk in love, and allow God to open doors for you. He will!

See, God is looking out for you. He wants you to succeed, and He knows the best path for you to follow. You won't miss out on any promotions or successes as long as you follow Him and let love be your guide. —MMA

POWER PRAYER

Lord, I trust You with my career. I know that You will cause me to succeed. I love You. Amen.

THE CONSULTANT ENIGMA

"Now go; I will help you
speak and will teach you what to say."

EXODUS 4:12

I remember when my company invited consultants to review our work procedures and make recommendations for how to improve them. In frustration, I listened to them make the same suggestions that the employees had been making for years. "Yes, that's exactly what we need to do!" management cheered, nodding like bobble-head characters in a car window.

Of course, bosses aren't the only ones who miss when important things are said. God faces this all the time. He continually speaks to us, showing us how we can work and minister better. He just needs us to listen.

If it's been awhile since you've heard God's voice, then take the time to listen to Him. If you're having trouble getting started, try listening to praise music, closing your eyes and focusing on the lyrics. Then begin praying—giving thanks, making your requests, and sitting quietly in His presence as you listen to those suggestions and impressions that He speaks to your heart. As you make this a habit, you'll find that you are more peaceful, productive, and in tune with Him than ever. –GM

POWER PRAYER

Dear Lord, I want to hear Your voice and follow Your will. Help me to develop my prayer time so that I can hear You clearly.

THE BALANCING ACT

Fight the good fight of the faith.
1 TIMOTHY 6:12

Balancing your commitment to your faith and your work can sometimes be difficult. At times your bosses or clients may question your commitment to your job, or they may honor your coworkers for achieving success even though it meant lowering their ethics or living for their jobs.

I've experienced this and struggled against the pull to be more like my peers. Though I was committed to my job, I was more committed to my convictions and my family time. Unfortunately, those traits aren't always honored in business, but in the end, I appreciated the peace of mind that my faith gave me. For me, the trade-off was worth it.

If you're finding it difficult to balance your convictions and your job, don't let yourself get frustrated. Don't doubt yourself. Follow the truth, fighting the good fight of faith that you know is right—the truth and peace of mind that only Jesus gives. Then trust Him to promote you and give you favor. You won't be disappointed. –GM

POWER PRAYER

Lord, thank You for giving me this job. I commit to follow You with all my heart, regardless of the pressures others try to place on me. Help me to see the value in the stand I take and not doubt Your truth.

IF I'M WONDER WOMAN,
WHERE'S MY INVISIBLE JET?

He gives strength to the weary
and increases the power of the weak.

ISAIAH 40:29

Michelle, I'm going to need you to work
late again tonight," my boss says, poking
his head into my office.

I grimace.

"Is that going to be a problem?" he asks,
eyebrows raised.

"No, sir," I answer, dialing my husband to see if
he can pick up the children from day care.

Is this a familiar scenario? If so, I feel for you.
It's tough to juggle all of the balls that are thrown
at you daily, isn't it? There are some days when I
just want to yell, "Calgon, take me away!" But
in reality, I'd have to bring my wireless laptop

computer into the tub with me if I were to squeeze a relaxing bath into my schedule. Life is busy— especially for the working woman. We're expected to bring home the bacon, fry it up in a pan, serve it, clean up the dishes, work out so the bacon doesn't deposit on our thighs, and do it all again the next day.

If you're feeling weary today, turn to God. No matter what you are facing. No matter how overwhelming it seems. No matter how tired you feel. God can help you. He will give you strength. Just ask Him. –MMA

POWER PRAYER

Lord, renew my strength. Help me to accomplish all that is on my plate. I love You. Amen.

LOVE THEM ANYWAY

"A new command I give you: Love one another.
As I have loved you, so you must love one another."
JOHN 13:34

It was happening again. The company needed a
scapegoat, and my friend was the latest victim.
While heating up my lunch in the company
microwave, I overheard my boss's plan to fire
my friend. As my boss discussed the particulars
with another department head, I felt sick inside.
I wanted to stand up on top of the lunch table
and say, "Liar, liar. Pants on fire." Everything they
were saying about my friend was untrue. Still,
she received the pink slip the next Friday.

After witnessing that fiasco, I had absolutely
no respect for my boss. My flesh wanted to talk
about her with my coworkers. I wanted to tell

them how she'd sold out to protect her own job. But the Lord reminded me that she was still in authority over me and I had to honor her. And because I was a Christian, I had to love her. Ugh! That was a tough one.

Maybe you have a boss who is hard to respect. If you're struggling today, ask God to let you see your boss through His eyes. You don't have to like your boss, but you do have to love your boss. Why not start today? —MMA

POWER PRAYER
Lord, help me to love my boss the way that You do. Amen.

There Ain't Enough Room for the Two of Us

For God is not a God of disorder but of peace.
1 Corinthians 14:33

Have you ever been in a situation where you felt so strongly that you were right, yet you were unable to voice your opinion because of your lack of authority? It's tough, isn't it? There have been times I have almost bitten clean through my tongue just to keep myself from speaking.

Difficult as it is, we have to honor those in authority over us. That doesn't mean we have to agree with our bosses all of the time, but we do have to show them respect. See, God is a God of order— not a God of confusion. To come against those in authority over us would never be God's way.

Need more convincing? Read Numbers chapter 12. Miriam and Aaron didn't like it when Moses, their leader (and brother), married a Cushite woman, and they talked badly about him. Well, the Lord heard them, and the Word says, "The anger of the Lord burned against them." And there were some serious consequences.

So if you're feeling badly toward your boss, ask God to forgive you. And if you truly feel that the leaders in your company are going in the wrong direction, pray for God to change their hearts. But don't come against them. Bite your tongue, and walk in peace. –MMA

POWER PRAYER
Lord, help me to honor those who are in authority over me. Amen.

SMILE!

A cheerful heart is good medicine,
but a crushed spirit dries up the bones.

PROVERBS 17:22

For those wanting to change their image in the workplace, here's some simple advice: Smile. Though it sounds simple, just walk through your office and see how many people consistently look bored or irritated. Then consider which coworkers you would trust with a new assignment or turn to in a pinch—probably those with a good attitude.

I've known several workers who desperately wanted a promotion, but they went through their days looking like they hated their jobs and sucked a lemon to prove it. They never smiled, and if you imposed on them in the slightest way. . .well, just forget about it. You wondered if they were going to slash your tires in the parking lot. The sad thing was that most of them just didn't know how to express themselves in a positive way. If they had just smiled and taken a more positive approach to their jobs, they probably would have been trusted with much more.

The Word says, "A cheerful heart is good medicine." Happiness is a choice. So if you're looking for a way to improve your standing in your office and enjoy your life in general, then take this one simple step: Smile! –GM

POWER PRAYER
Lord, thank You for giving me my job, and help me to have a good attitude as I do it.

THE GOLDEN RULE
OF GETTING AHEAD

"So in everything, do to others
what you would have them do to you."
MATTHEW 7:12

E ver worked retail? I worked my way through
college as a clerk in a large department
store. It wasn't a glamorous job, but it paid the
apartment rent and allowed me to buy cool
clothes at a discount. That was good.

You know what else was good? I learned that
the term "working on commission" really meant
making a sale any way possible to reach your sales
quota. This created a friendly (and sometimes not
so friendly) competition among coworkers.

We didn't use the "it's your turn" method.
Nope, this store's philosophy was simply "move in
before your coworkers and make the sale." So that's
what I did. But I soon learned that when I made
my quota, I didn't make any friends. I was ruthless.
I knew I wasn't "doing unto others as I wanted
them to do unto me." So I stopped pushing and

simply allowed God to open up sales opportunities for me. And He did.

See, God can help you make your sales quota, and you won't have to sacrifice your salvation to do so! Trust Him to help you achieve your goals, and you won't have to step on anyone's head to get ahead. —MMA

POWER PRAYER

Lord, help me to be sensitive to others as I move up the corporate ladder. Amen.

Tending the Sheep

From that day on the Spirit of the LORD
came upon David in power. . . .
But David went back and forth from Saul
to tend his father's sheep at Bethlehem.

1 Samuel 16:13; 17:15

Everyone knows that David was a great leader,
but at the beginning of his life—when he was
out tending sheep—he didn't really look like one.
He was the youngest of seven brothers, probably
picked on by the older ones and given the chores
that no one else wanted to do. That's when God
chose him to be king. God saw David's potential
even though David didn't ascend to the throne
until much later. From the time that Samuel
anointed him until he became king, David worked

as a professional musician and then as a military warrior. And even then, he still tended sheep. He wasn't exactly on the fast track.

You may find that even though God calls you to do something, it'll take patience and perseverance for it to happen. You may know that you're going to have your own company or a higher position, but, until then, allow God to equip you for that position so you are prepared for it. Through patience and perseverance, you can see your plans fulfilled. –GM

POWER PRAYER
Lord, thank You for preparing me for Your plans. I submit to You in all I do.

Big Picture

Where there is no vision, the people perish.
PROVERBS 29:18 KJV

I've learned from some wonderful bosses how important it is to continually keep the vision of a project in front of a team. In fact, the most successful projects that I've ever been a part of have been when everyone knew the goal and her place in bringing it to pass.

Even in our everyday lives, having a vision is vital. I've met many women who struggle with knowing the vision God has for their lives. They jokingly say they want to know what they're going to be when they grow up—regardless of their age.

Though it may sound simple to do, discovering your life's goal can be challenging. Sometimes it takes time for the pieces to come together, but don't get discouraged. Be faithful to what He's put in front of you right now. Continue to pray, read His Word, and talk to your pastor or mentor. As you do, you'll eventually see the pieces come together. You'll understand that God was preparing you, even when you felt like you were just spinning your wheels. Never doubt that He has a vision for you! –GM

POWER PRAYER

Lord, thank You for directing me in every area of my life. I ask that You give me a clear vision of what I should do now and in the future.

FOR EVERYTHING
THERE IS A SEASON

There is a time for everything,
and a season for every activity under heaven.

ECCLESIASTES 3:1

I wish I could say that I lived for change, that I was one of those remarkable people who thrive on learning new procedures and think a fun Saturday afternoon includes rearranging the living room furniture. Unfortunately, that gift passed me by.

Of course, I don't absolutely hate it. Sometimes I change the pillows on my sofa, if that counts.

Change can be uncomfortable, especially change in the workplace. When change comes, take a deep breath. God is still in control. Step back and objectively ask yourself if the change is good. Has it been carefully thought out? Is the goal to help the office function more smoothly?

Are your managers supporting it 100 percent? If the answers to some or all of these questions are yes, then it's time to jump on board. If you have concerns—and it's appropriate—voice them. But once the decision has been made, become a team player and make the most of the situation. Your submission and positive attitude will be appreciated by your coworkers and, more importantly, by God. –GM

POWER PRAYER
Lord, I understand that there is a time and season for everything. Since change is difficult for me, I ask for Your help to be a positive influence through it.

Nurturing the Blooms

Lazy hands make a man poor,
but diligent hands bring wealth.

Proverbs 10:4

One of my favorite hobbies is gardening. I love planning flower beds, choosing plants, and even spending an afternoon in the garden. While I garden, I think about my work and relationships. It's relaxing, yet challenging. I have to imagine what the garden will look like in one

to two years. Then, once I do the initial work, I nurture the plants so they can thrive. I have to be diligent if I want to enjoy the benefits of my work.

This is a fast-food world where results are expected quickly, and diligence is sorely under-developed. But often it takes diligence to see the fruit of your labor. It takes time and effort to excel. A smart boss won't hand over the largest accounts to someone who hasn't proven herself to be a hardworking employee. He wants someone he can trust.

There are some qualities with which people are born, but others—like flowers in a garden—have to be nurtured. Decide to develop the quality of diligence in your life. In the end, you'll enjoy the colorful, lush benefits of your hard work. –GM

POWER PRAYER

Lord, thank You for all that You've given me in my life. I'm thankful for it, and I will be diligent in everything I do—my family, my work, and my relationship with You.

I Want My Old Job Back

*In all your ways acknowledge him,
and he will make your paths straight.*

PROVERBS 3:6

I stood in the grocery checkout line, reading the headlines of the *National Enquirer* when suddenly my thoughts were interrupted by a conversation behind me.

"I don't know why that Michelle Adams person has to write all of that garbage in the newspaper," the woman said. "We don't need to know that stuff."

As the two women continued bashing my reporting skills (insulting everything about me except my mother), I tried not to hyperventilate. I paid for my groceries and quickly escaped, wondering why I was being persecuted for simply doing my job—reporting on the school system's scandal.

I had recently been promoted from city government reporter to education reporter, and this was my first big story on that beat. Unfortunately, it wasn't a very flattering story for the community, and I wasn't gaining any popularity points. I suddenly longed for my boring city government beat. It was much safer there.

Change is difficult—even if the change is a promotion! Change comes with situations we've never encountered before. That's why we have to trust God and lean not on our own understanding. We may feel unsure and void of answers, but Jesus is the Answer. So trust Him and He will direct your paths. –MMA

POWER PRAYER
Lord, help me to trust You no matter what changes I encounter in life. Amen.

LIVIN' FOR THE BELL

But our citizenship is in heaven.
And we eagerly await a Savior from there,
the Lord Jesus Christ.

PHILIPPIANS 3:20

There are days when even the most dedicated employee is "livin' for the bell." You just can't wait until the end of the day or the end of your shift. You may not even consider yourself a clock-watcher, but on the difficult days or when you have something important to do after work, you pack up five minutes early and bolt when the time comes.

As Christians, there is another bell that we should eagerly await: the return of our Lord Jesus Christ. The apostle Paul understood a great truth—his real home was in heaven. And with all that he did, he still wrote that he "eagerly awaited" Jesus' return. Though it can be difficult to imagine Jesus' return in today's world, it isn't any less of a reality, and we shouldn't be any less eager for it.

As you continue going about your business, don't forget to eagerly await the Lord's return. Remember that as important as anything you do here on earth may be, heaven—your true home—awaits. –GM

POWER PRAYER
Lord, help me to remember You in everything I do.
I recognize Your lordship in my life and in this world,
and I realize that this earth is not my true home.

Rubies, Gold, and Short Skirts

Charm is deceptive, and beauty is fleeting;
but a woman who fears the LORD is to be praised.
PROVERBS 31:30

Recently, I watched a reality TV show where several young professional women were competing for a promotion. They were trying to land accounts and increase sales. Sadly, they were relying on their sexuality to be successful, flirting with potential clients. They were trying to get ahead based on something other than their talents.

It made me wonder if I had ever tried to get ahead with cheap tricks rather than the talents God has given me. Had I flirted with manipulation or not telling the "whole" truth to make my way to the top? I hope I haven't, but it made me think how easy it is in the workplace to resort to bending the rules of integrity rather than using the talents God has given us.

As God's daughter, you don't have to rely on cheap tricks to get ahead. You can rest in Him, knowing that God has given you every talent and ability you need to succeed. You can keep His standard of holiness and be "a woman who fears the Lord." –GM

POWER PRAYER

Lord, thank You for loving me. I accept Your love and desire to be a woman who fears and loves You.

Help! I'm Surrounded by Yes-Men

"God is with you in everything you do."
Genesis 21:22

Do you work in a company where you're surrounded by yes-men? You know the type. The boss says, "I think it would be a good idea if we all get our hair cut in Mohawks." And suddenly, every person in the room says, "Absolutely. I've always wanted a Mohawk— it's my favorite hairstyle! Mohawks rule! Why didn't I think of that?"

Ahh! It makes you want to run out of the conference room screaming, doesn't it?

Every time it happens, the rebel spirit in me wants to stand up and say the exact opposite—

even if I agree with the popular consensus. It's even more upsetting if you know in your heart of hearts that the yes-men are enthusiastically backing a wrong decision.

Let's face it. Working in the midst of brown-nosers and yes-men is never easy. It's hard to stand up for what you believe—especially when you're the only one willing to have an opinion that differs from the boss. But don't despair. You don't have to go it alone. God will be your ally. And, even if it's just you and Him against the world, that's all you'll ever need. –MMA

POWER PRAYER

Lord, help me to have the courage to speak my mind,
and help me to do so with respect and tact. Amen.

My Pinto
versus Your Lexus

"What have I accomplished compared to you?
Aren't the gleanings of Ephraim's grapes better than
the full grape harvest of Abiezer?"

JUDGES 8:2

She was everything I wanted to be. I looked across the newsroom at her, and I wondered how she was able to write award-winning stories, parent such wonderful children, and remain a size 4. I admired her, and yes, at times I was jealous of her—especially when I started playing the comparison game.

Ever played that game?

At first, it seems quite harmless. You simply admire a coworker. But if you take it a step further, you'll be sorry. That's when you start wondering, *Why can't I do my job as well as she does hers? How does she afford such wonderful suits?* From there, it's a downward spiral. By the time you hit the bottom, you dislike your coworker and you can't stand yourself.

I've got three words for you: *Don't Go There!* The next time the devil whispers in your ear, *See Carol over there? She earns ten thousand dollars more a year than you, and she is two sizes smaller!* tell him to back off. Begin praising God for who you are through Him, and thank Him for the plans He has for your life. They are awesome—just as awesome as Carol's. I promise! –MMA

POWER PRAYER
Lord, help me to stop comparing myself to others and become happy with who I am in You. Amen.

It Goes a Long Way

So then, just as you received Christ Jesus as Lord,
continue to live in him,
rooted and built up in him, strengthened
in the faith as you were taught,
and overflowing with thankfulness.
Colossians 2:6–7

Have you worked around people who complained constantly? They didn't like the boss's decisions or the company's policies or the receptionist's attitude. Everything was a problem; nothing was easy. Their complaints were like nails on a chalkboard. All they had to do was start talking, and everyone around them cringed. Needless to say, they didn't win any Miss Congeniality awards.

Every office has challenges, but having someone constantly point them out is draining.

You'd rather be around positive people who are thankful for their jobs and peers.

Thankfulness goes a long way toward developing a positive attitude. It shows that you acknowledge that God is in control and works through, or sometimes in spite of, the people around you. So develop an attitude of thankfulness, realizing that it'll help you become a favorite among your peers and strengthen your relationship with the Lord. –GM

POWER PRAYER

Lord, I thank You for Your provision. I thank You for the job You've given me and the people You've placed around me. I trust You in all I do.

GIVE IT YOUR ALL—
NO MATTER WHAT

"I know, my God, that you test the heart
and are pleased with integrity."

1 CHRONICLES 29:17

Be honest: Do you work a little harder when you know your boss is looking over your shoulder? Do you slack off a bit when you know the boss is on vacation?

If you answered yes to either of those questions, I'd say you're not alone. It's a natural instinct to work a little harder in order to impress those in authority over us, yet God wants us to do our best even when nobody is watching. God wants us to walk in the utmost integrity.

That means, even if your coworkers are surfing the Internet when they're supposed to be working, you resist that temptation and do your assignments instead. That means, even if everyone around you steals office supplies, you leave those paper clips and notepads in your office. That means, you give 110 percent whether your boss is in the office or out of town.

Do your best every single day, and watch God work. Sow integrity, hard work, and loyalty; and reap a great harvest. God will cause your hard work and your integrity to gain your boss's attention. And you can rest assured that your Boss in heaven is taking note, too. –MMA

POWER PRAYER

Lord, help me to work to the best of my ability—
no matter what. I love You. Amen.

WALK IN LOVE

Love is kind.

1 CORINTHIANS 13:4

Happy birthday, Michelle!" shouted three of my closest coworkers. They had decorated my office and sprinkled it with fun-sized chocolate candy bars. They knew I'd need an extra lift. After all, it was my thirtieth birthday. I had been dreading it for weeks. Leaving behind my twenties was a tough one. I feared that crow's-feet were

just around the corner. But my buddies were there to cheer me up—except for Claire.

As I headed downstairs for my morning Diet Coke, she stopped me in the hallway. "So how old are you today?"

"I'm thirty," I whispered.

"Really?" Claire said, raising her eyebrows. "I thought you were *way* older than that."

With that curt comment, she took her size-4 body down the hall, leaving me feeling deflated and miserable. She was great at spewing hurtful comments on a daily basis. Oh, how I longed to say some zingers back at her. I had crafted them carefully in my mind, just waiting for the right time. But whenever that opportunity arose, the Lord wouldn't let me speak. I kept hearing that inner voice saying, *"Walk in love."*

Maybe there's a "Claire" in your office that you'd like to throttle. Well, don't. Instead, kill her with kindness. Walk in love. Yes, it's difficult but you don't have to walk it alone. God will help you. –MMA

Power Prayer

Father, help me walk in Your love. Amen.

JUST SAY NO

Pride goes before destruction,
a haughty spirit before a fall.
PROVERBS 16:18

Do you have trouble saying no to your superiors? I have a classic case of "Sure, I can do that," even though I know I'm saying yes when I should be saying no. For instance, last summer I signed two book contracts with a deadline of September 1. When both publishers asked if I needed more time, I proudly said, "No, I can totally meet that deadline." I didn't want to admit that I needed more time. I was afraid they might see it as a sign of weakness and lose confidence in me.

So I practically killed myself to meet those deadlines. I even ended up having to ask for an extension on one of the deadlines! Ugh. I learned that one the hard way.

Looking back, I realize it was fear and pride that kept me from being honest with myself and my bosses. I was afraid of disappointing anyone, and I was too proud to admit that I couldn't do what they were asking me to do.

Maybe you're on that same merry-go-round today. If so, jump off! Ask God to help you say no when no is the needed answer. And ask Him to help you swallow your pride and admit when you need help. There's no shame in being human. —MMA

POWER PRAYER
Lord, help me to walk free from fear and pride. Amen.

An Affair to Avoid

"You shall not commit adultery."

Exodus 20:14

D id you know that workplace affairs account for 80 percent of all marital infidelity? That's a startling statistic, isn't it? Most affairs start off very harmless. A man and a woman become friends because they are coworkers. Soon they begin to have lunch together—alone. The woman begins confiding in her male coworker. In turn, he also shares intimate details with her. Suddenly, they become quite attracted to one another. Soon the two are emotionally involved. This, of course, leads to the physical relationship. Eventually, they both leave their spouses and children—tearing up two families. And it all started with a few harmless lunches. Amazing, isn't it?

Unfortunately, the above scenario is far too common. There may be an office affair going on where you work right now. You may even be taking part in one. If you are involved in an office romance, nip it in the bud. Run away from your coadulterer and into God's arms. God will forgive you.

If you are happily married and thinking, *I would never do such a thing,* just heed this warning: Be careful. Don't be flirtatious at work. Don't have lunch alone with a male coworker. Ask God to make you sensitive to dangerous situations. Let your conscience (Holy Spirit) be your guide. –MMA

POWER PRAYER
Lord, help me to be sensitive to actions that might promote an office affair. Amen.

The Choice

I have learned the secret
of being content in any and every situation,
whether well fed or hungry,
whether living in plenty or in want.
I can do everything through him who gives me strength.

PHILIPPIANS 4:12–13

Paul is a great example of someone who chose to be content. Though he was imprisoned for preaching the gospel and his surroundings were filthy, he continued to teach other Christians through his letters. In fact, while he was in prison, he wrote: "I have learned the secret of being content in any and every situation." He knew that his personal comfort wasn't as important as his eternal calling. What a challenge for everyone!

Regardless of what position you have now or in the future, you are first called to be a child of

God and a light to the world. Though it isn't wrong to pursue promotions, you need to realize that true happiness and contentment doesn't come because of outward circumstances. It's a choice—one you make every day.

As you work at your job—one you may love or hate—choose to be a light for Jesus. Through your attitude and work ethic you could be more of an example and blessing to one of your coworkers than you could ever know. –GM

POWER PRAYER

Lord, I choose to be content today. I know that, more than anything else, I'm called to be a light for You.

The Squigys in Our Lives

He has made everything beautiful in its time.

ECCLESIASTES 3:11

Close to my home is a small park with winding trails and a small creek. It's a slice of the country right in the middle of the city, and I love to walk through it. Along the way, I count the animals I come across—raccoons, snakes, birds, frogs, and my personal favorites: turtles. There is one small turtle in particular that I look for each time. I've affectionately named him Squigy.

Often, as I search for him, other park goers have rushed past me, oblivious to anything else. It makes me wonder: How often have I rushed by God's handiwork because I was too hurried to appreciate it? As busy as we are in our lives, it's easy to miss God's beauty—spring wildflowers, giggling children, and, yes, even small turtles.

Today, take time to appreciate the beauty around you—in nature and in people. There will always be a project due or meeting to attend, but a year from now, will you really remember it?

Don't be so focused on your work that you lose sight of the Squigys. In the end, the small beauties—the Squigys—will probably be what you remember most. –GM

POWER PRAYER
Lord, thank You for the beauty that You've placed around me. Help me to appreciate those beauties every day.

JESUS' LEADERSHIP STYLE

"You've observed how godless rulers throw
their weight around, how quickly a little power goes to
their heads. It's not going to be that way with you.
Whoever wants to be great must become a servant."

MATTHEW 20:25–26 MSG

When some people get a little power,
it's scary. Unfortunately, many feel that
when they attain power, they'll finally get the
respect they deserve or be able to make the
changes that they want.

In actuality, leadership and respect aren't one
and the same. Surely you've known bosses,
possibly the one you have right now, who didn't
have the respect of their subordinates. Given the
opportunity, their employees would sell them
down the river for a smile and a wink because
instead of building up their team, they lead
by intimidation.

In Matthew 20:25–26, Jesus responded to a mother's request that her two sons hold powerful positions in heaven by saying, "Whoever wants to be great must become a servant." Regardless of what position you hold, develop an attitude of servanthood. Don't think of yourself more highly than others or look for chances to intimidate people. As you develop Jesus' leadership style, you'll be a leader others will respect and want to follow. –GM

POWER PRAYER

Lord, help me to become a godly leader who has an attitude of serving others. Whatever position I hold, I want to honor You.

If I'm the Employee
of the Month, Everyone
Else Must Be on Vacation

He said, "If I have found favor in your eyes,
my lord, do not pass your servant by."

GENESIS 18:3

Michelle Adams to the Marketing Conference
Room, please."

As I heard the page over the company PA
system, I wondered, *What have I done?* I hadn't
parked illegally in weeks. I hadn't been late that day.

I took one deep breath and entered the conference room where a dozen of my coworkers, my
boss, and my director all stood.

Suddenly, they started applauding.

"Michelle, I just wanted to congratulate you
in front of your peers on a job well done," my
director said. "That is the best annual report I've
ever read."

It was official—I was the Golden Child of the moment. I felt so good.

That feeling of elation lasted about two days. Then, for reasons unknown to me, I couldn't even write my name with any accuracy in my supervisor's eyes. What had changed? I was the same writer that had written "the best annual report ever" just days before!

My Golden Child status left as quickly as it had arrived.

You see, you can easily fall out of favor with man, but you can't fall out of favor with God. So even if you're not the Golden Child at your company, you're a Golden Child with your heavenly Father, and that's more than enough. —MMA

POWER PRAYER
Thank You, Lord, for loving me unconditionally. Amen.

There's Not Enough of Me to Go Around

I can do everything through him who gives me strength.
PHILIPPIANS 4:13

Did you ever walk on a balance beam when you were a child? I loved gymnastics when I was growing up, but I was never very good on the balance beam. I'd topple off to one side quite often. You know what's ironic? I'm still having trouble with that whole balancing concept. Only now I'm having trouble balancing my personal and professional life. How about you?

Maybe you're an employee, a wife, a mom, a friend, a daughter, a sister, an aunt, a church volunteer, etc. And you're not sure how to be all of those things at one time. If you are all those things, welcome to the Sisterhood—the "Sisterhood of There's Not Enough of Me to Go Around."

There are days when I wonder how I am supposed to accomplish everything that is on my plate. But you know what? *I'm* not! God never intended me to do this by myself. And He never intended for you to go it alone, either. The Word tells us that we can do all things through Christ who gives us strength. *All* means *all,* right? So no matter how many roles you're fulfilling today, don't sweat it! God will help you. –MMA

POWER PRAYER

Thank You, Lord, for giving me the strength and wisdom to stay on the balance beam of life. I know I can do all things through You. Amen.

ONE-UPMANSHIP

For where you have envy and selfish ambition,
there you find disorder and every evil practice.

JAMES 3:16

Ever worked with someone who always one-ups you? Uh-huh, you know the type. If you have an idea that will save the company hundreds of dollars, she comes up with a plan to save thousands. Irritating, isn't it?

Be honest. That old green-eyed monster occasionally rears its ugly head when she enters the room. Jealousy is a funny thing. It sort of sneaks up on you when you least expect it. And unfortunately, it brings a few of its friends like anger, frustration, and strife. Let's face it—that's no way to live.

Instead of focusing all of your energy on the "one-upper," turn your attention to God. Ask God to help you see her through *His* eyes. Ask Him to fill you up with so much love that there won't be any room for jealousy, anger, frustration, or strife.

Be happy when your coworker succeeds. Rejoice with her, because until you can celebrate her accomplishments, you'll never have any success of your own. Remember, God is no respecter of persons. What He has done for her, He will also do for you—if you'll keep your heart right. –MMA

POWER PRAYER
Father, please help me to get along with all of my coworkers. Change my heart, Lord. I love You. Amen.

You Can't Win 'Em All

"But I tell you: Love your enemies
and pray for those who persecute you."
MATTHEW 5:44

I was a senior in college, working in the Misses Designer Clothing section at a large department store. I needed the job to pay for college expenses. I was young and full of enthusiasm, high ideals, and big dreams—all of which really irritated my thirty-something boss. Just when I thought I'd won her over, I found out differently. I was in one of the stalls in the ladies' room when my boss and another department head came in to fix their lipstick.

"I have to figure out a way to get rid of Michelle," my boss whispered. "She drives me crazy. She's just so bright-eyed and bushy-tailed. Maybe I can transfer her to Men's Accessories."

I was the only Michelle in her department. I was crushed. I stayed in the stall until they left, had a good cry, and took my post back at the cash register. I learned a hard lesson that day: Not everyone in the workforce is going to like you—no matter how hard you try. If you're dealing with persecution at work, begin praying for those who are deliberately being mean to you, and watch God change your situation. He will. —MMA

POWER PRAYER

Lord, I pray for those workers who are being mean to me right now. And I thank You for vindication and favor. Amen.

Ouch!

He who ignores discipline comes to poverty and shame,
but whoever heeds correction is honored.

PROVERBS 13:18

Now we come to a subject that no one likes to talk about: correction. It's definitely up there with submission and gluttony in the "Christian Principles We'd Like to Ignore" category.

I know. I know. None of us likes to admit we're wrong. We like to believe that we're either right or at least that we've made the best decisions with the information we had available. Translated: It wasn't our fault. We all make mistakes or errors in judgment.

The great thing is that as Christians we aren't beyond hope. As my pastor loves to remind us,

"Nothing is fatal or final in Jesus." So then why is it so hard for us to turn around and admit when we're wrong?

Is it pride? Maybe.

Conviction? Sometimes.

Whatever the reason, you have to remember to graciously accept correction—from God and leaders. Even when you may not totally agree, you need to respectfully accept their decisions. Not only can it make your work life easier, but as Scripture reminds you, "Whoever heeds correction is honored." Now isn't that a good thing? –GM

POWER PRAYER

Lord, help me to remain humble and to respectfully accept correction.

Run Your Own Race

Let us throw off everything that hinders
and the sin that so easily entangles, and let us run with
perseverance the race marked out for us.

Hebrews 12:1

H ave you ever looked across the conference
table, stared your supervisor in the eyes,
and wondered, *Just how, may I ask, did you ever
advance to that position?* C'mon, be honest.
Sometimes it's tough to be respectful when you
know the person you call "boss" knows less than
you do. It's even more difficult if your boss rose to
that position through office politics, nepotism, or
via another unfair avenue.

But, hey, that's not your concern.

You shouldn't waste precious time dwelling
on such things. Instead, keep your eyes on God.
Like the Bible says, run *your* race. Don't worry
about anyone else's race. Keep your heart right.
Pray for your boss. Then just do your best at
your position.

You may have been treated unfairly. You may have been looked over for a promotion you deserved. You may work for a boss who treats you badly. You may have been at the company way longer than your current boss. But don't let it get to you. Just run your race. God already thinks you are a winner. —MMA

POWER PRAYER
Thank You, Father, for my job. Keep my heart right, Lord, in the midst of nepotism and office politics. Help me to be respectful of those in authority over me. Amen.

THE GREAT UNKNOWN

Fearless now, I trust in God;
what can mere mortals do to me?

PSALM 56:11 MSG

As much as the fear of failure can hinder us, the fear of success can hold us back, too. This is a difficult fear to overcome because the end results are unknown. You know what's expected in your current position, and the thought of leaving it leaves you scared and nervous.

The only way to rid yourself of any fear is with the Word of God. By studying the Word of God and discovering what God says about you, your faith in Him will increase. You'll begin to view the obstacles in your career as small in comparison to Him.

So if you're struggling with the fear of success, take time to read and meditate on God's Word.

Find the Scriptures with which you can relate, copy them down, and put them in a place where you can see them every day—your Bible, your desk drawer, your purse. Don't just read them like you're reading your grocery list; read them as though they are personal words from your heavenly Father. Continue to pray, and surround yourself with positive Christian friends who will encourage you. With all this, you're sure to succeed. –GM

POWER PRAYER

Lord, as I meditate on Your Word, I trust You to fulfill Your plan in my life and to help me follow that plan without fear.

Does This Cubicle
Come in a Bigger Size?

I am not saying this because I am in need, for I
have learned to be content whatever the circumstances.

Philippians 4:11

Recently I heard a preacher say you should enjoy the journey on the way to where you're going. I wish I'd known that truth when I first started my career as a reporter for a daily newspaper. My first writing gig? I was hired as a police beat reporter. I had to work long weekday hours and most Friday nights. I desperately wanted to work in a different area of the newspaper—anything but the police beat. I spent so much time dreaming about a new assignment that I didn't enjoy the one I had. I took for granted that I was able to hang out with the cool sports guys on

Friday nights. I took for granted that working on Friday nights allowed me to work side by side with the managing editor. I took many things for granted.

Looking back, those days were critical to my development as a writer. God had placed me in that job for a season. It wasn't my "dream job," but before the dream job could manifest, I had to learn some stuff. Maybe you're in that "learning stuff" place today—on the way to your dream job. If so, hang in there. Be content where you are. Enjoy the journey. –MMA

POWER PRAYER
Lord, help me to enjoy the journey. Amen.

New Kids on the Block

The end of a matter is better than its beginning,
and patience is better than pride.

ECCLESIASTES 7:8

God bless new bosses and coworkers. They're in a tough place. They've just walked into new positions, not knowing the office history or procedures. They come with their own experiences and expertise. Many times, they've been hired to bring about change by improving productivity or sales.

For those who work with them, it can be challenging. You've done your job to the best of your ability within the boundaries of the current organization, possibly carving out your own niche, only to have a newcomer decide to change everything. Your instincts tell you to resist the person and her ideas, because everything's been working just fine until now, right?

Remember that not all changes are bad. When Jesus came into your life, He made *big* changes. He completely changed the way you thought about your life. The ideas in His Word may have seemed foreign, but they worked—even better than you could have imagined.

So when that newcomer comes into your office, be patient. You never know. . .her ideas may improve things, too. –GM

POWER PRAYER

Heavenly Father, please give me patience and insight to work with the new people who come into my office. Help me to listen to and discuss their ideas clearly and sensibly.

Putting the Golden Rule to Work

"So in everything, do to others
what you would have them do to you."

Honestly, bosses have a tough time of it. Yes, there are those who only pay lip service to serious issues or get a thrill out of flexing their authoritative muscles, but most bosses try to do a good job. They walk a fine line between being too lenient and too harsh. They need to get a job done while preventing their natives from becoming too restless, and they're held accountable for the work of every person under them.

At one time or another, I think everyone has been critical of their boss. As unfair as it may be, employees can demand perfection from their boss while expecting mercy with regard to their own work. A double standard, to be sure.

Scripture says to "do to others what you would have them do to you." Remember this in regard to your boss as you go through your week. If you don't want your boss to expect perfection from you every day, then you really can't expect perfection from him, either. He's in a tough place, and in addition to your good work, he needs your support and understanding. –GM

POWER PRAYER

Lord, I want to be a support to my boss this week and show favor toward him. Show me how to do that.

SURVIVING THE BOYS' CLUB

Refrain from anger and turn from wrath.
PSALM 37:8

Have you ever heard the saying "A woman has to be twice as good as a man to receive half as much credit"? I don't believe this is true in all situations, but I do believe that in some offices there is still a stigma against women. A woman can say the same thing that a man says, but the man's opinion carries more weight.

Though some women are bitter about this, as Christians we need to guard against the bitterness. And we can take comfort that the tide is changing; not all male coworkers and bosses can be lumped into the boys' club mentality. Yes, it may still exist, but getting spiteful won't solve anything.

Only through sharpening your skills and praying will you succeed in a "boys' club" business. Learn from the successful women in your organization or industry. Trust God to show you how to be effective, and then rest in the knowledge that you're doing all that He's told you to do. Yes, it may still be a man's business world, but with perseverance and faith, you can succeed. —GM

POWER PRAYER

Lord, help me to be the best employee that I can possibly be. I want to be successful in the position that You've given me, and I trust that You'll show me the steps to take in order to do so.

PUNCTUALITY

There is a time for everything,
and a season for every activity under heaven.
ECCLESIASTES 3:1

Punctuality. Just writing the word is painful to me. I've never been very good at being on time. It's not that I don't give myself ample time to get ready. It's just that I try to do too much before I leave the house. For instance, I'll get ready and head for the door, and then I'll remember that I need to switch the laundry. Next thing I know, I'm off to another late start.

I once worked in an optometry office for a very kind doctor. He never yelled about my 8:05–8:10 arrival. Instead, he pulled me aside one day and said,

"Listen, I don't care if you're a little late. But some of the other employees are upset about it. So just try to be on time." As they say in Texas, I felt lower than a snake's belly. I realized that my tardiness was creating stress for my wonderful boss, and it was ruining my Christian witness. I asked God to help me change that very day.

If you're challenged with punctuality, ask God to help you. He wants to be involved in every part of your life. Go ahead and talk to Him. He's got the time. —MMA

POWER PRAYER
Lord, help me to be on time. I want to be a good witness for You. Amen.

Out of Balance

By the seventh day God had finished
the work he had been doing;
so on the seventh day he rested from all his work.

GENESIS 2:2

When Friday night rolls around, are you exhausted? Have you given so much at work that week that you have nothing left to give to your family and friends? If you answered yes to either question, you might be a workaholic.

While you should give your company 110 percent when you're on the job, if you take mounds of work home or you're constantly on your cell phone fielding questions from clients, you've crossed over into the land of workaholics.

It's a tough call. You want to be the "go-to gal" when your boss is looking for someone to promote. So if that means taking work home, you're willing to do it—but at what expense? If your job is stealing time away from your family, your friends, and your God, then you're out of balance.

And you know what happens when we're out of balance? We fall on our hind ends.

So take time today and ask God to help you get your life in balance. He will! He is the great prioritizer. Follow His example. He worked hard for six days and rested on the seventh. We should do the same. –MMA

POWER PRAYER

Lord, I'm asking You to put my life in balance. I love You and trust You. Amen.

Out for Blood

"Love your enemies, do good to those who hate you,
bless those who curse you, pray for those who mistreat you."
LUKE 6:27–28

Janet was very unhappy in her job, and I had to work with her. She disagreed with management and thought she knew how the office should be run. Though she was angry with management, she decided to take her hostility out on me.

Wherever I turned, her accusations followed. Several times, she questioned my integrity. Unfortunately, whenever I tried to defend myself, people looked at me as though I were guilty. Eventually, months later, I was vindicated when she left the company, but it was still a bad situation. I felt like I was one of Cinderella's ugly stepsisters in a parallel universe.

It would be wonderful if everyone played by the same rules, but some people are just out for blood. Maybe you stand between them and a promotion. Maybe you have favor with management, or maybe you're just the nearest victim. Whatever the reason, situations like that don't usually go away by themselves.

If you have a coworker who is out for blood, pray for her. Be wise and follow God's advice to "bless" her. Eventually the truth will rise to the surface. –GM

POWER PRAYER

Lord, You know the truth about this situation. I am determined to bless this person, and I ask for Your wisdom as I deal with her.

GETTING NOTICED

As it is, you boast and brag. All such boasting is evil.
JAMES 4:16

We all know "Brenda Brag-a-lot." She seizes every opportunity to share all about her successes. There's at least one "Brenda" in every company. She's easy to spot because she is always talking, and those surrounding her have expressions on their faces that say, "We really don't care. Why don't you take a personal day or something!"

In this dog-eat-dog world, many feel the need to brag on themselves. They believe the old adage, "If I don't look out for number one, who will?" Well, God will! You don't have to toot your own horn to move up in your company. God will cause you to outshine others, and you won't even have to open your mouth.

The Bible says that God has crowned you with glory and honor and favor. He will give you favor with your bosses and your coworkers. He will cause your efforts and accomplishments to get noticed by the "powers that be." God will do that for you. All you have to do is ask, and then thank Him for it every day! Don't become a "Brenda Brag-a-lot." Let God do your bragging for you. He loves to dote on His children! –MMA

POWER PRAYER

Thank You, Lord, for giving me favor with my bosses and coworkers. I praise You that my accomplishments will not go unnoticed. Amen.

Solitaire

Agree with each other,
love each other, be deep-spirited friends.
PHILIPPIANS 2:2 MSG

You've probably heard of companies that have removed the game of solitaire from their computer systems because too many employees wasted time. If you're like me, the thought of someone spending their workday playing solitaire sounds pretty ridiculous.

Unfortunately, many people play "solitaire" at work—and I'm not talking about with computers. They play solitaire by trying to accomplish everything themselves and avoiding working with groups. If they're put on a team, they feel like they're beating their heads against the wall because other workers just can't do the work as well as they could alone—or so they believe. Sound familiar? Effectively working in groups doesn't always come easy. It's a practiced art, but a group can accomplish more than a single person.

Just as you aren't meant to go it alone at work, you shouldn't try to go it alone in your spiritual life. God wants you to have relationships with other Christians. Together, you'll accomplish more for Him than you would alone. So the next time you cringe when joining a group, take time to appreciate all you can do together. As you work toward a common goal, you'll see the benefits in the outcome. –GM

POWER PRAYER
Lord, thank You for the coworkers You've place around me. Help me to be a positive team player with them.

NOBODY LIKES ME

*You made him a little lower than the heavenly beings
and crowned him with glory and honor.*

PSALM 8:5

Whenever I used to have a feel-sorry-for-myself day, my mother would sing this silly little song: "Nobody likes me. Everybody hates me. Guess I'll go eat worms."

How about you? Have you felt like eating a big, fat juicy worm lately? Are you feeling sorry for yourself? Do you feel as though you'll never be able to succeed in your job? If you answered yes to any of those questions, you need to give your insecurities to God and ask Him to replace them with confidence and supernatural favor.

Here's what the Bible says about you in Deuteronomy 28:13: "The Lord will make you the head, not the tail." I like being the head; how about you? And John 12:26 says, "My Father will honor the one who serves me." Did you get that? God will honor you! So stop feeling badly about yourself.

Start thinking, feeling, believing, and saying what God says about you; and pretty soon others will think highly of you, too. It works! But you have to walk in it every day. C'mon, now. Put down that big juicy worm, and start walking in God's divine favor. It's the only way to walk! –MMA

POWER PRAYER
Lord, replace my insecurities with Your kind of confidence. Amen.

PASSED OVER

The LORD is a refuge for the oppressed,
a stronghold in times of trouble.
Those who know your name will trust in you,
for you, LORD, have never forsaken those who seek you.

PSALM 9:9–10

When I graduated college, I interviewed for five different positions in one company, and yet I kept losing the positions to other people, some of whom were much less qualified. During that three-month period, I worked in a temporary position, just waiting for something—anything— to open. Then, right before my temporary commitment was over, a vacancy came open in a great area. I went from feeling like a wallflower to feeling very blessed. Looking back, I saw how faithful God was—He made sure I got the best possible job.

If you've been passed over for a job, don't get discouraged or doubt your worth. You are valuable, and God is still working on your behalf. He hasn't forgotten you and though you may not be able to see it now, He has your best interest at heart. So don't give up on Him—because He certainly hasn't given up on you. –GM

POWER PRAYER

Lord, Your Word says that You will never forsake those who seek You, and that's just what I'm doing. You are my refuge during this difficult time and I trust You.

The Power of Words

Those who love to talk will experience the consequences,
for the tongue can kill or nourish life.
PROVERBS 18:21 NLT

As a former sportswriter for a daily newspaper in southern Indiana, I love sports—especially college basketball (Go Hoosiers!)—but I'm also quite partial to golf.

I recently saw a special on the Golf Channel about golf legend Gary Player. In this interview, Player said that from the time he took up golf at age fourteen, he would wake up, look himself in the mirror, and say, "I'm going to be the best golfer in the whole world." It's no wonder that in 1965 at age twenty-nine, he won golf's Grand Slam—the Masters, the U.S. Open, the British

Open, and the PGA Championship. At that time, he was the youngest competitor to ever reach that pinnacle. How did he do it? He saw himself as a winner and a champion long before his talents merited such talk. He understood the power of words, vision, and dreams.

Do you understand the power of words? Why not learn from Gary Player? Wake up each morning and look yourself in the mirror and say: "Everything I touch prospers and succeeds. I am well able to accomplish the task that God has put before me." Speak words of victory, and you'll experience victory in and out of the office! —MMA

POWER PRAYER

Lord, help me to only speak words of victory. Amen.

What Light?

*"Record the vision
and inscribe it on tablets,
that the one who reads it may run."*

Habakkuk 2:2 nasb

Have you ever felt so discouraged in your job that you just wanted to crawl under your desk, eat some chocolate, and cry? I think we've all been there. On those days, my mother would always say, "Into each life a little rain must fall," or "This, too, shall pass," or "There's a light at the end of the tunnel." All three statements are quite true, but when you're right smack-dab in the middle of a discouraging day, it's hard to see that promised light at the end of the long tunnel.

Well, I have some good news for you—Jesus is the Light! And He is there for you right now. No matter how desperate your situation at work may seem, the Lord can deliver you from it. No matter how hopeless you feel, Jesus can restore your hope and your vision today.

Grab some notebook paper and write your vision. Write the dreams that God has placed in your heart. Like the Word says, keep that vision before you. Stick it inside your planner, or tuck it away in your desk drawer. Don't let discouragement rob you of your vision. Come out from under your desk, and run with your vision today! –MMA

POWER PRAYER

Thank You, Lord, for restoring my hope and vision today. Amen.

Fellow Texans MICHELLE MEDLOCK ADAMS and GENA MASELLI are both full-time writers. Michelle, a former award-winning newspaper journalist, now writes magazine articles, women's devotionals, and children's picture books. Visit Michelle at www.michellemedlockadams.com. Gena, who spent ten years developing materials for worldwide Christian ministries, now writes devotionals, nonfiction, and magazine and Internet articles.

Scripture Index

Old Testament

New Testament